S0-CEY-993

Copyright 1974 Gerald Clayton

Published by Gerald Clayton, 112 College Street, Camborne, Cornwall, England, TR14 7LA, in association with Edisud, La Calade, Aix-en-Provence.

All rights reserved. Reproduction in all forms, including photocopies and computer storage, forbidden.

Looking and Cooking
in Provence

Vielle rue, Villefranche, Cote D'Azur, France.

Weights and Measures

Metric to English

Solids

1 kilogramme = approx 2 lb 3 oz

500 grammes = approx 1 lb $1_{1/2}$ oz

250 grammes = approx 9 oz

100 grammes = approx $3_{1/2}$ oz

50 grammes = approx $1_{3/4}$ oz

Liquids

1 litre = $1_{3/4}$ pints (35 fl.oz)

500 cc. = $_{3/4}$ pint + 4 tblspns

250 cc. = 9 fl.oz

100 cc. = 3 fl.oz or 6 tblspns

10 cc. $\doteq$ 1 dessertspoon

Metric to American

Fat or butter

1 kilogramme = approx 4 cups solidly packed

500 grammes = approx 2 cups solidly packed

250 grammes = approx 1 cup solidly packed

100 grammes = approx $_{1/2}$ cup solidly packed

50 grammes = $3_{1/3}$ tablespoons

Sugar

1 kilogramme = approx $4_{1/2}$ cups

500 grammes = approx $2_{1/3}$ cups

250 grammes = approx 1 cup plus
4 tablespoons

100 grammes = approx 5 tablespoons

Sieved plain flour

1 kilogramme = 9 cups

500 grammes = $4_{1/2}$ cups

250 grammes = 2 cups

100 grammes = about 5 tablespoons

Liquids

1 litre (1000cc) = 1 quart plus 6 tblspns

500 c.c. = approx 2 cups

250 c.c. = 1 cup plus 1 tablespoon

100 c.c. = approx 6 tablespoons

Looking

Cooking

Herbs

Basil (Basilic) : A very aromatic herb which lacks bitterness. Use in soups, sauces, and omelettes. Very good indeed with tomato dishes and salads.

Bay leaf (Laurier) : Widely used, one or two leaves at a time, in casseroles and soups.

Bouquet garni : The most-used of all herbal additions to casseroles, stews and soups. Tie together a bay leaf, two or three sprigs of parsley and a sprig of thyme. Remove at the end of cooking.

Fennel (Fenouil) : Often used in fish dishes, including soups. Sprigs are often inserted into cuts in the flesh of mullet and other fish being grilled. The sprigs catch fine and impart a powerful aroma to the fish.

Marjoram (Marjolaine) : Extremely aromatic, useful in casseroles and marinades, often with rosemary and thyme. Can be very sparingly used as garnish on salads.

Parsley (Persil) : The chopped fresh leaves and minor stalks make a splendid garnish for patato and other salads. Also widely used in tomato dishes, vegetable soups, and with fish.

Rosemary (Romarin) : Use this one sparingly, for it is very pungent. Extremely good with lamb, also for use with pork and fish dishes. If you use a sprig of fresh leaves remove at the end of cooking, for the leaves are spiky in the mouth.

Sage (Sauge) : Often used with veal, also with pork. Be very careful with it, for the flavour can easily drown all others in the dish.

Tarragon (Estragon) : Often called the prince of herbs. Usually encountered in tarragon vinegar for use on salads but the chopped fresh herb is delightful in omelettes, as part of the fines herbes, and is very good with chicken.

Thyme (Thym) : Like many other good things, best used a little at a time ! Excellent in marinades and casseroles.

Côtelettes d'Agneau

Lamb chops done this way are a good example of how a little imagination and a little trouble can transform a cut of meat which is invariably grilled or fried unadorned..

I like to serve this with a plain green salad dressed in lemon juice.

To serve four :
8 lamb chops,
3 onions, finely chopped,
1 cup of buillon,
1 tablespoon of flour
Butter,
Half glass of boiling milk
1 clove of garlic, cut with knife,
3 egg-yolks. Salt. Breadcrumbs.

La Vieille Ville, Menton

Gently fry the chops in butter but do not overcook. Remove from the pan and place under weight to coll.

Melt a little butter in the pan and add the buillon. When it simmers, add the onions and cook gently for about 20 minutes.

In another pan melt a knob of butter, stir in the flour and allow to bubble for a few seconds, then add the boiling milk quickly, stirring all the time, until the sauce thickens. Add the onions, season with salt, and remove the pan from the flame when all are well blended.

Place the chops on a fireproof dish or tray that has been lightly greased. Stir the beaten egg-yolks into the sauce, pour it over the chops, sprinkle all over with breadcrumbs and bake in a medium oven until the crumbs are browned.

© 1980 Gerald Clayton · Le Pont D'Avignon et Palais des Papes

Strictly speaking, aioli is the sauce alone, and the French nickname of "Beurre de Provence" is a sly dig at the Provençal fondness for garlic.

In Provence itself it has come to mean a complete meal of white fish, eaten cold with cold boiled potatoes, carrots and onions, a little salad for garnish, and washed down with a bottle of chilled rosé wine. On a hot summer's day it is a superb meal.

These days the sauce is made by pounding cloves of garlic in a mortar until pulpy, and for a third of a litre of sauce I recommend 12 cloves. (Most cookbooks are too cowardly over the amount of garlic).

You then add two egg yolks, a pinch of salt, and add olive oil a drop at a time, beating all the time, just as for mayonnaise. When the oil starts to thicken, increase the rate of pouring to a thin stream.

Make sure that neither the eggs, oil nor bowl are cold. If the sauce goes curdled, break another yolk into a separate bowl and add the mixture a drop at a time.

A very old recipe uses garlic, oil alone, and thickens the sauce with breadcrumbs.

Frankly I see no reason why you can't cheat over the garlic by using dried garlic powder (ail moulu). Put a couple of teaspoons of it in a cup, cover the powder with just enough water, and let it stand for two minutes, then add your egg yolks.

Porte de Sainte Anne, Orgon f.c.

For the vegetables, either use new potatoes boiled in their jackets or old ones cut in half.

Use whole new carrots or old ones cut in two, and with them boil whole medium sized onions.

Cooking all the veg together in a steamer is even better.

Lettuce and a few sliced tomatoes add colour.

The fish may be whatever you fancy, preferably poached or steamed, but it could be baked in the oven. At any rate, it is eaten cold, like everything else.

Le Moulin de Daudet, Provence

Daube de Bœuf Provençale

An exact recipe for a daube de bœuf Provençale is difficult to give because there are hundreds of minor variations, many of them passed on from mother to daughter, father to son.

However, this version is one I have found satisfactory, though I do vary it from time to time.

Make the marinade a day before you cook the dish.

To serve four :

1 kilo of stewing beef such as chuck steak, or even shin.

2 rashers of bacon, cut up. In France, use "poitrine salée".

2 onions, chopped.

12 black olives.

For the marinade :

1 sliced onion.

2 sliced carrots.

2 crushed cloves of garlic.

1 bay leaf.

Sprig each of rosemary, thyme and marjoram.

1 ou 2 tablespoons red wine vinegar

2 large glasses red wine

1 thin strip of orange peel (not treated with chemical preservative)

Vielle Rue S°RASSE

Make up the marinade, cut the beef into inch cubes, lay it in the marinade and turn a few times.

Turn it again that evening, and again the following morning.

Start cooking the dish by frying the bacon, cut into pieces, for a few minutes, then add the chopped onions for a further few minutes.

Now take the meat from the marinade and brown it with the bacon and onions for a minute or two.

Add all the marinade, heat gently to boiling point, cover the pan and allow to simmer very slowly for about three hours.

Add the olives, allow to heat through, and serve.

Forum de Cardeurs, Aix-en-Provence.

Pernes-les-Fontaines, Vaucluse

Œufs aux Anchois

This little dish is very tasty, and makes an excellent hors d'œuvre or cocktail snack. It may also serve as a light lunch or supper.

To serve six :

6 hardboiled eggs

1 onion, chopped finely

1 large tomato, chopped and with seeds removed.

12 fillets of anchovy

Lemon juice, pepper, bay leaf

Butter for frying

Slice the eggs in half lengthways and remove the yolks.

Fry the onion and tomato very gently in butter for about ten minutes. Season with pepper, add the bay leaf and also add the eggyolks after mashing them with a fork. Now add the pounded fillets, and continue to cook gently until most of the liquid has been absorbed.

Miscard the bay leaf, sprinkle the mixture with fresh lemon juice and pass through a sieve.

Arrange the stuffing in the eggwhites so that it forms slight mounds.

La Grande Rue, Les Baux, Provence

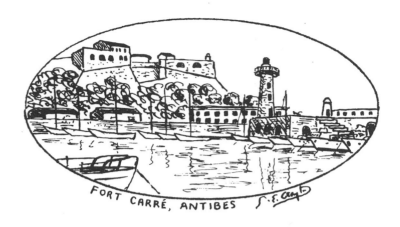

FORT CARRÉ, ANTIBES

Pissaladière

The rectangles of commercially baked pissaladière hawked around the old town in Nice, and sold by innumerable bakeries in the area bear little resemblance to the real thing except that they are smeared with fried onion and may possibly have a suggestion of anchovy, if you are lucky.

It is perfectly proper to make this dish with shortcrust pastry instead of pizza dough, and indeed is better made so if you wish to eat it cold as an hors d'œuvre.

To serve four :

125 grammes plain flour

60 grammes hard margarine or half and half margarine and lard

Water to bind, and a pinch of salt

6 large onions, chopped

12 black olives

12 anchovy fillets

4 tablespoons of olive oil

Mix pinch of salt with the flour, and cut in the fat with a knife, then rub with fingertips till it resembles crumbs. Keep a light touch.

Bind with enough water to make a good clean ball of dough = by which I mean that if you roll it around the side of the mixing bowl all the pastry comes away cleanly.

Roll out thinly and line a greased baking tray, raising the edges slightly.

Fry the onions gently in oil for 20 minutes, but do not allow to go very brown. Allow to cool.

Prick the pastry all over, spread the onion evenly across, arrange the anchovies in a lattice pattern, and dot with olives. Bake for 30 minutes in a medium oven.

La Ponche, St. Tropez, Côte D'Azur

Les arènes, Arles

Pommes de Terre au Lard

Like so many other peasant dishes, this one is substantial, tasty, easy to prepare, and economical. It is very good served with boiled carrots and a simple green salad, pleasing both to the eye and palate.

To serve four :

200 grammes lean bacon

Large onion, chopped finely

5 or 6 tomatoes, chopped

1 kilo or less of potatoes

Little flour or cornflour

Bouquet garni. Fresh parsley

Olive oil or butter

Half pint stock, water, 1 glass of white wine or a small tot of brandy

1 clove of garlic, chopped

Cut the bacon fairly small, melt the butter, or heat the oil in a pan and add bacon and onion.

Cook for five minutes then add the tomatoes. Season with salt and pepper, add the stock or water and wine or brandy, and the garlic.

Now throw in the bouquet garni and the potatoes, which should be quarted or sliced, depending on their size.

Boil the potatoes, but not too furiously, until cooked. This will be about 20 minutes.

If necessary, stir in a little flour or cornflour to thicken the liquid. This may not be necessary, it depends on the type of potato.

Finally, remove the bouquet garni, stir in a handful of fresh parsley and serve with salad.

Les Martigues

Rue Waldeck Rousseau, Cavaillon

Poule au Riz au Safran

Somewhat different from most casseroles of chicken, this one is enhanced by the golden colour of the saffron rice and the unusual sauce.

To serve four :

1 hen or chicken

2 onions, each stuck with 2 cloves

1 onion finely chopped

2 carrots, sliced across

2 tomatoes, chopped

1 stick of celery, chopped

250 grammes long-grain rice

2 egg yolks, beaten

Juice of 1 lemon

1 glass white dry wine

1 litre water or stock

2 cloves of garlic

Bouquet garni

15 stamens of saffron

Pepper, salt, flour, butter

Put the bird in a saucepan with cloved onions, carrots, celery and tomatoes, add herbs, wine, stock and seasonings, bring to boil, cover, and simmer gently till bird is cooked. (1 hour for chicken, 90 minutes for a hen).

30 minutes before end of cooking, put knob of butter in another pan, melt, add the chopped onion, fry gently for a few minutes. Now add the rice, stir a few times, and add half the liquor from the chicken.

Bring to boil, adjust seasonings if desired, add the saffron, and allow to cook till all the rice has risen to absorb the liquid. Make sure it does not burn.

In a third pan make a roux by melting a knob of butter and stirring in the flour, allow to bubble for a few seconds, then add the rest of the stock from the chicken. Stir continously while heating until sauce thickens. Season again if desired, remove from flame, stir in the beaten egg yolks and lemon juice. Serve the chicken on the rice after removing bouquet garni and saffron, and pour the sauce over the chicken.

La Vieille Fontaine, St. Paul-de-Vence

Le Suquet, Cannes.

Poulet Grillé
à la Niçoise

Niçoise cuisine contains virtually no chicken dishes, so this one, invented in recent years by Mère Besson, widow of a well-known Niçois chef, and herself now owner of a restaurant in Cannes, makes a welcome addition to the repertoire. I found it to be delicious, and the chicken itself is also superb eaten cold as a picnic dish.

To serve four :

1 plump chicken, jointed.

4 to 6 tomatoes, peeled and sliced or chopped.

4 to 6 cloves of garlic, sliced

250 grammes tender French beans

100 grammes black olives

Butter, olive oil, fresh parsley

French mustard, salt, pepper

Season the chicken pieces with salt and pepper, spread them liberally with mustard, then either grill them, or better still, bake them in the oven.

Meanwhile fry the tomatoes and garlic gently in oil, season to taste, and add the olives when cooking is just finishing.

In a separate pan sauté the beans gently in butter.

When serving, garnish the chicken and tomatoes with a sprinkling of fresh parsley. Serve with chips on the side.

La Fontaine du Peyra, Vence.

G. E. Clyt

Chapelle de St. Sixte, Eygalières, Provence.

Ratatouille

One of the most famous vegetable dishes in the world, ratatouille is a perfect example of the Provencal genius for taking everyday ingredients, and in a simple way, combining them to create something which is quite unmistakeable.

To serve six :

2 medium onions, sliced thinly

3 medium sized aubergines (eggplant)

1 sweet green pepper and one sweet red pepper

500 grammes pelled tomatoes

500 grammes courgettes

3 large cloves of garlic, chopped

1 teaspoon each of rosemary, thyme, marjoram and sweet basil

Olive oil, salt, pepper

Gently fry the onions on a low flame in about three tablespoons of olive oil. Meanwhile chop the tomatoes roughly, slice the unpeeled courgettes and unpeeled aubergines crossways, remove the core and seeds from the peppers and cut into thin strips and inch or so long.

Add all the vegetables to the pan, with the garlic, salt and pepper. Turn to coat with oil, cover the pan, and fry gently for about 30 minutes.

Remove the lid, add the herbs, and fry uncovered for a few minutes longer until most of the liquid has been driven off, leaving the mixture just moist.

LA TREILLE

Vieux · Nice

S.E. Clerc

Salade Niçoise

Some of the recipes for this most famous of all salads, even in eminently reputable books, would make a broad bean blush.

Boiled potatoes, for exemple, lettuce, and even beetroot, figure in some of the versions I have come across.

In fact salade Nicoise is a supreme example of a dish which writers muck about with, trying to give a 'new twist' to it, until eventually it is distorted into a travesty of the original.

No cooked vegetable of any kind should appear in a salade Nicoise, nor should lettuce.

Escoffier was born at nearby Villeneuve-Loubet, but his own version was perhaps a little too severe. It consisted of tunny fish, anchovies and tomatoes, garnished with tarragon, chervil and chives.

He had, however, grasped the essential point of simplicity, but locally, black olives are always included.

Vieux Roquebrune

The tunny fish should be flaked, and the anchovy fillets chopped. The tomatoes should always be quartered, never sliced.

It is also considered quite proper to include some or all of the following : Tender young raw broad beans, slices of cucumber, quartered hard-boiled eggs. To avoid an unsightly green ring around the yolk, plunge the eggs into plenty of cold water immediately after boiling for six minutes.

Traditionally, the dressing is of salt, pepper and olive oil, but for those who dislike neat oil, I think vinaigrette is more acceptable.

Villefranche, Cote d'Azur

Tarte aux Pommes à la Genot

St. Réparate, Vieux Nice

Making an apple tart with halved or quartered apples stood 'on end' was taught me by M. Genot Otto=Bruc, of Nice. He rightly maintains that cooked this way, the apples retain much more flavour than if laid out in the more usual thin slices.

To serve four non=slimmers :

125 grammes plain white flour

70 grammes butter

1 tablespoon sugar

Water to bind

Enough eating apples, peeled, cored and halved or quartered, according to size, to cover a 10 =inch plate stacked 'on end'

Several handfuls of caster sugar

Cut the butter into the flour with a blunt knife, then rub with the finger tips, lifting hands above the bowl, until the mixture is crumbly. Do this as quickly as possible. Add the sugar and mix well.

Now add water a little at a time, mixing in with the knife until it looks doughy. Knead it with the fingers until you have a ball of dough which comes away cleanly without 'sticking' to the bowl. Take care not to 'overwork' the dough.

Roll out the pastry, trim to fit round a greased flan tin. Arrange the apples in circles to fit closely, drench with handfuls of caster sugar and bake in a medium oven for 30 or 40 minutes.

Eze Village

Le Barroux

Tomates Farcies

Many cookery books give what are alleged to be repices for Tomates Farcies Provencale, but most of them are pretty insipid concoctions, the chief ingredient of the stuffing being either bread or rice. This recipe admittedly has bread in it as a filling, but many other good things besides, and it is far and away the best recipe I have encountered. It is a genuine old Provencale recipe, and makes an excellent hors d'œuvre, a light luncheon dish, or a very tasty supper snack.

To serve four :

10 large ripe tomatoes

2 chopped onions

100 grammes bread soaked in water

2 cloves of garlic, chopped

Bunch of fresh parsley, finely chopped

100 grammes boiled beef, veal or ham

2 egg yolks. Salt and pepper

Olive oil

Cut the tops from eight tomatoes and remove the insides, sprinkle the cases lightly with salt.

Heat a little oil in a pan and gently fry the onions then add two chopped tomatoes.

Allow to continue cooking for a few minutes then add the soaked bread, the meat, garlic and parsley.
Season with salt and pepper.

Remove from the flame and stir in the beaten egg yolks. The mixture should be firm but elastic. Stuff the eight tomatoes, replace the tops, sprinkle well with olive oil, and bake in a hot oven for 20 to 30 minutes. The cases of the tomatoes should be well browned, but not, of course, charred too much.

Notes

Notes

Achevé d'imprimer
sur les presses de Cronion S.A.
à Barcelone
en juin 1992.
Dépot légal à parution.

Imprimé en Espagne